30-DAY DEVOTIONAL

Becoming GOD'S
Dwelling Place

One scripture at a time

by
Athena C. Shack

Published by Watersprings Publishing, a division of Watersprings Media House, LLC.
P.O. BOX 1284
Olive Branch, MS 38654
www.waterspringsmedia.com
Contact publisher for bulk orders and permission requests.

Copyrights © 2020 by Athena C. Shack

All rights reserved. No part of this publication may be reproduced, distributed, or transmitted in any form or by any means, including photocopying, recording, or other electronic or mechanical methods, without the prior written permission of the publisher, except in the case of brief quotations embodied in critical reviews and certain other noncommercial uses permitted by copyright law.

Scripture quotations are taken from the Holy Bible, New International Version®. NIV® Copyright 1973, 1978, 1984 by International Bible Society. Used by permission of Zondervan. All rights reserved.

Scripture quotations marked "NKJV" are taken from the New King James Version. Copyright © 1982 by Thomas Nelson, Inc. Used by permission. All rights reserved.

Printed in the United States of America.

Library of Congress Control Number: 2020915690

ISBN-13: 978-1-948877-68-8

Table of Contents

	Introduction	1
DAY 1	Dig to be Nourished	4
DAY 2	Set for the Kingdom	7
DAY 3	Access Granted	10
DAY 4	Built to Dwell	13
DAY 5	Godvine Fruit	16
DAY 6	Much Fruit	19
DAY 7	I'm Turning Back	22
DAY 8	A Vigilant Posture	25
DAY 9	The Righteous	28
DAY 10	Entry to the Holy Place	31
DAY 11	Guard!	34
DAY 12	The Key to Our Place	37
DAY 13	Approved Worker	40
DAY 14	Surgery of the Heart	43
DAY 15	A Dwellable Diet	46
DAY 16	Slay	49
DAY 17	Joy Through it All	52

DAY 18	Training for Service	55
DAY 19	The Guard	58
DAY 20	Melody of My Heart	61
DAY 21	Dwellable	64
DAY 22	The Condition	67
DAY 23	The Difference	70
DAY 24	Covered and Safe	73
DAY 25	Spirit Fed, Spirit Fueled	76
DAY 26	Identify	79
DAY 27	Generational Dwelling Place	82
DAY 28	Overcomer	85
DAY 29	Transformed	88
DAY 30	Rooted in Love	91
	About the Author	93
	Other Books by the Author	94

Introduction

It was just a few days before the Thanksgiving holiday and my family and I were preparing the house for a very important guest. My mom. She was flying in to stay with us for a few days for the holiday. The kids, hubby, and I embarked on our extra, good cleaning. You know when you dust, clean, and attend to the neglected spots in the house. We decluttered the areas that often get overlooked during our typical, hustle-bustle days, which is everyday of the week. I know we are not the only family that has the holiday cleaning ritual in prepration for guests. We want the people who are invited into our homes to not only feel welcome, but comfortable. Isn't that what we expect when we are staying overnight in someone's home or a hotel? We expect that the same preparation to take place before our arrival.

Can you imagine being an invited guest into someone's home and there aren't any preparations for your stay? The house is a mess, you can't find a place to lay down your luggage because there are piles of clothes, toys, and shoes all over the floor. Dirty dishes have piled up in the sink, casting a strong odor of last week's dinners. Not a pleasant picture, huh? *(Insert my Caribbean accent here.)* Not quite inviting, eh? However, the same case can be made in our spiritual lives. We invite God into a messy space that we have left unprepared for His stay within our daily lives.

As believers of Christ, we know that God is a refuge, a place we can go to be safe because God is our dwelling place. But can we be God's dwelling place? Can God be invited into our dwelling place?

#dwellhere

We make space occastionally, especially on Sunday's or our typical worship day. However, to dwell, means to occupy, to stay, to live in that space. God's place will always be dwellable for you. Your heart, and your home should be just as dwellable for God to stay, not just visit. Becoming a dwelling place for God means that we are occupied by God's Spirit, not our flesh, nor the world. It also means that we are consistenly making preparation for the living God to live within us. **God wants to be our dwelling place.** God wants to live in us but our lives must be conducive to His presence - daily!

This is what God placed on my heart while I was developing the topical scripture writing/prayer journals, Write. Listen. Pray.™ What began as a journal has expanded into this devotional. The method that I use for my devotional time, is the same one I used for the writing of this devotional. Daily, I take one scripture, write it down, circle, underline, and/or define words looking for deeper or new revelation, especially if it's a popular scripture. Then I meditate on it, write what I hear and allow God to speak to me. Lastly, I pray the heart of the scripture and I start my day God-centered and God-dwellable.

As God has placed this devotional in my heart for the body of Christ. My prayer is that you will discipline yourself over the next 30 days to hear God's heart through these scriptures and words of exhortation, then recite each prayer out loud. My hope is that you will prepare yourself daily to be a dwelling place for God. If you miss a day, it's okay, just get back on track, get back in the Word of God and invite God into your space with these words: "dwell here."

#dwellhere

DAY 1

Today's Scripture

COLOSSIANS 2:6-7, NIV

So then, just as you received Christ Jesus as Lord, continue to live your lives in Him, rooted and built up in Him strengthened in the faith as you were taught, and overflowing with thankfulness.

#dwellhere

Dig to be Nourished

Many of us, when we started this Christian race, ran quickly. We ran with zeal; we grew in strength and our faith increased. Then, we hit a plateau and became comfortable with a status quo life.

Fortunately, stagnancy and complacency cannot abide in God's dwelling place. If we want God to live in us, we must continually dig into the depth of His Word. When we dig into God's Word we become rooted in the righteousness of God. God's seed germinates in our hearts and bears fruit in our lives.

We must allow God's spirt to do the building so we can do the living. Whenever roots are nourished it produces healthy and vibrant fruit, and this warrants a thankful heart. Let's dig! Be rooted and strengthened to a life that's not stagnant but overflowing with thankfulness. God can most certainly dwell in a heart full of gratitude.

#dwellhere

DAY 4

Today's Scripture

ACTS 17: 24, NIV

The God who made the world and everything in it is the Lord of heaven and earth and does not live in temples built by human hands.

To dwell, shrine, temple

#dwellhere

Pray the Word

Gracious God our Father, even when I don't feel worthy enough to be in Your presence. I know that I have an audience with You. In all my imperfections, You still love me. You consistently call me and keep me near Your dwelling place. Thank You for never leaving me, abandoning me, nor forsaking me. Thank You for the instruction through Your Word that teaches me and guides me to Your place – that dwelling place. My prayer is that my life, my heart, and my lips will become and/or remain worthy of the access You have granted me to Your dwelling place. I shall dwell with You all of my days. Dwell in me Lord, in Jesus' name.

My Affirmation

I shall dwell!

#dwellhere

Access Granted

God's dwelling place is a place of refuge, safety, refinement, healing, restoration, forgiveness, and a place of promise for you and me. Our God is Lord! When you allow God to be your Lord, you have special access to God's dwelling place. Think about how amazing it is that WE get to dwell in God's place because He is our Lord! That is a privilege and a promise. Me, you, and we get to dwell in the presence of the Lord – the Almighty God, the Creator of heaven and earth.

Even though we are flawed and unworthy at times, we can find a dwelling place in the Lord. It's not because of our goodness, but it's because of God's grace. Access is given to those who believe and put their trust in the living God. A heart that believes, also obeys, also praises, and worships the living God. It is indeed a loving opportunity, to be granted access to God's dwelling place.

DAY 3

Today's Scripture

PSALM 84:1, NIV

How lovely is your (dwelling) place,

Lord Almighty!

A residence; also, a temple, tabernacle.

#dwellhere

Pray the Word

God, I thank You for the opportunity to be a Kingdom citizen. I will exercise my mind to be focused on the Kingdom and things above. Forgive me for every wasted moment or activity that has distracted me from my Kingdom assignment.
I pray that my mind shifts from my external to-do-list to my eternal to-do-list. I pray that my thinking reflects Your plan and will for my life.
I will be obedient to Your Word and to Your voice. I will set my mind on Your purpose, Your goodness, Your faithfulness, and Your righteousness. God You alone are worthy of all the glory and my attention. Thank You for allowing Your presence to be my eternal dwelling place. Dwell with me on earth so that I may dwell with You in heaven. In Jesus' name I pray, Amen.

My Affirmation

I am a Kingdom citizen!

#dwellhere

Set for the Kingdom

Albeit brief, this scripture reminds us of at least two things. First, with all the distractions and to-do-lists of life that spin uncontrollably in our minds, we need to unplug more consistently. Unplug, the technology, media, voices – good, bad, or indifferent to become quiet and still enough to hear the sound of our own heartbeat.

Secondly, it reminds us that we are Kingdom citizens and that we live here on earth, but we shouldn't let our location determine our mindset. To "set" means to exercise our mind. We are always going to have to be intentional with the "setting," because it won't come easy. However, we should *desire* and *will* to set, or be careful with our mind. If our mind is set, correct, and established on God's things, then our earthly life won't simply be busy, but more purposeful and set on God's assignment for us in the earth. Let's face it, it's easy to become distracted but it's not an excuse to stay that way. Our breath is on earth, but our life is in heaven. You are a Kingdom citizen! Your mind should reflect your eternal dwelling place.

#dwellhere

DAY 2

Today's Scripture

COLOSSIANS 3:2, NIV

Set your minds on things above, not on earthly things.

To be mentally disposed – be careful. To exercise the mind.

Pray the Word

God, it is my responsibility to dig into You and be built up in You, be strengthened in the faith and overflow with thanksgiving. Forgive me for every time or season that I was not rooted. Forgive me for the times that I waivered in my faith, became self-absorbed, worldly, and ungrateful. Cleanse me from all unrighteousness and implore me to dig further into Your word. Daily, I will seek Your face, seek Your voice, and seek Your Word so that I may be built up in You. You are God, my Father, dwell here.
In Jesus' name I pray, Amen.

My Affirmation

I will dig!

#dwellhere

Built to Dwell

God made the world and the heavens and earth. He made all creation and chooses not to live in something that was made by what He created. Why would our God want to live in something that was fabricated for humans by humans? God made us and desires to live in us, not a box, not an ark, and not a church building. We, humans, are the Church, the Ecclesia, the community of believers. We are the place where God can live in the earth, not a building crafted with bricks and wood. We are to be a temple, a dwelling place worthy enough for God to dwell within. Attending church doesn't qualify us or make us dwellable. We become dwellable by offering ourselves as a living sacrifice, holy and pleasing to God. While God does not dwell in fabricated buildings, God does dwell in us. Therefore, it is your responsibility to make yourself dwellable.

#dwellhere

Pray the Word

Gracious God, I understand in Your Word that You did not make temples to dwell in. You desire to dwell in Your people. My prayer today is that I would be dwellable. Search my heart God and find a place that Your Spirit can dwell. Cleanse my heart and remove anything that would prevent You from living on the inside of me. Help me to identify spiritual clutter, unrighteousness, destiny killers, or anything else that keeps me from being livable. Allow Your Spirit to live and move in me. Thank You for making me with the capacity to embody You. I will be holy, because You are holy, that is my earnest desire.
Dwell in me Lord, in Jesus' name.

My Affirmation

I am dwellable!

#dwellhere

DAY 5

Today's Scripture

JOHN 15:4, NIV

Remain in me, as I remain in you. No branch can bear fruit by itself; it must remain in the vine. Neither can you bear fruit unless you remain in me.

#dwellhere

Godvine Fruit

Consider for a moment what you look like apart from God. In order to stay spiritually healthy, you must be connected to God's vine. The vine is imperative for spiritual growth and nutrition. Apart from God, there is no good thing within us. When God is visible in you, then you are the you that God created you to be. God created you to be a living vessel that bears fruit that resembles Himself in us. You must remain in God, in order for God to remain in you. It's not a pleasant sight to see who we would be without God living in us. Truthfully, if we are not connected to God's vine and bearing God-like fruit, we are connected to something else. If we are connected to and feeding from ungodly branches, then surely, we will die. The stench and unpleasing sight of rotten, indigestible fruit is visible to both God and people. Child of God, stay connected to God's vine and bear the fruit of God's Spirit. Not only for you, but for those that eat from you as well.

Pray the Word

Lord, I want to remain in You, and You remain in me. Forgive me for all the times that I disconnected or turned away from You and impeded my growth in You. I only desire to grow Godly fruit and be a branch that others can eat from. Thank You for remaining in me during my moments of doubt, faithlessness, and brokenness. Thank You for never leaving nor forsaking me. Thank You for always running after me with Your loving kindness and mercifulness. God I shall remain in You and bear Godly fruit all the days of this life. Dwell here, in Jesus' name, Amen.

My Affirmation

I will bear God-vine fruit.

#dwellhere

DAY 6

Today's Scripture

JOHN 15:5, NIV

I am the vine; you are the branches. If you remain in me and I in you, you will bear much fruit; apart from me you can do nothing.

#dwellhere

Much Fruit

We are alive for a purpose. Our every breath is an indication of God's mercy and grace. Just think for a moment how long it took you to say yes to God. I'm referring to the yes that was followed by immediate obedience in spite of your comfort zone, doubts, or insecurities. I'm referring to the yes that produced good fruit. The time we have spent apart from God prior to salvation is covered by the grace of God. Through the extension of that grace we have the opportunity and responsibility to get it right and live right. Personally, I do not want to die with unfulfilled potential and purpose. I want to live and bear as much fruit as humanly possible. Therefore, we have two choices – to be in, or be apart. I think the choice is clear, but we have to make that choice every day in order to remain in God.

In order to bear much fruit, we have to have a healthy connection to the vine. Daily, not weekly, you must be intentional on doing the things that keep you connected to the vine that feeds your spirit so you bear much fruit.

#dwellhere

Pray the Word

God, everything that does not bear much fruit in me I don't want it inside of me. Forgive me for every time I failed to yield a harvest in my life. Forgive me for every time I hid from You, disconnected from You, or sinned against You. God teach me how to be sown in the dark, winter months so that I can peak and grow in good harvest times of my life. I will remain in You and stay connected to You because I desire to bear much fruit. Daily, I will read Your Word, pray, and be obedient to You as my only source for life. I declare from this day forward that I will always bear fruit, in season and out of season, because I'm connected to You. In Jesus' name. Amen.

My Affirmation

I am fruitful.

#dwellhere

DAY 7

Today's Scripture

JOHN 15:6, NIV

If you do not remain in me, you are like a branch that is thrown away and withers; such branches are picked up, thrown into the fire and burned.

#dwellhere

I'm Turning Back

People leave, people change their minds, people turn their backs on God. Sometimes hurt and brokenness will keep us away from God, God's Church, and God's Word. Some of us find our way back to God through life's hurts and disappointments, and others turn away forever. An apostate is someone that turns away from God and never turns back to God. This saddens me because this means they knew God and had some level of experience or exposure to God, but got turned around.

In this scripture, it is clear that if we do not remain in God we are cut off and burned which is an indicator of Hell as a final un-resting place. Whatever you are "feeling" about your situation it's not worth going to hell and your soul spending an eternity there. If your back has been turned away from God because of hurt, disappointment, disobedience, or sin, I implore you to turn back to our merciful God. Get back in the Vine, stay connected to God. Simply attending church does not indicate connection. Connection is when you become the Church and God lives in you.

#dwellhere

Pray the Word

God, forgive me for every time I turned my back, turned away from You, and turned toward sin. I could have so easily been cut off from You. Thank You for your mercy that kept me connected to You in every season of my life. God, I honor You, thank You, and praise You. I shall remain in You and You in me.
I shall live and not die and declare
the works of the Lord.
In Jesus' holy name I pray. Amen.

My Affirmation

I shall live connected to God.

#dwellhere

DAY 8

Today's Scripture

COLOSSIANS 4:2, NIV

Devote yourselves to prayer, being watchful and thankful.

A Vigilant Posture

As children of God, we have a mandate to pray. To devote or continue in prayer means to persevere, be earnest and diligent in prayer. In other words, not letting up or being slothful, lazy, and only praying when something is wrong. That's a defensive posture of prayer.

Prayer should not be an after-thought. It's a charge, a mandate from God that we would pray continuously. In prayer, we must be vigilant and watchful. To be vigilant is an offensive posture of prayer not a defensive posture. In this posture of prayer, we are initiating prayer daily, interceding for ourselves and God's people. We are inclining our ear to hear the heart of God and obtain direction. We are in front of the next problem and not praying because of a problem. When you devote yourself in prayer, you are always ready for what's next. Being devoted to prayer is being vigilant, watchful, and ready. In this posture we are positioned for God's grace, mercy, favor, and God's promises. I charge you today, to be consistent, be vigilant, and be thankful as your posture of prayer.

#dwellhere

Pray the Word

Eternal Father, thank You for Your Word that lives, and breathes. Thank You for this day and its mercies You have extended to us to get our prayer life in order. Forgive me for not having a consistent posture of prayer. I shall be vigilant, earnest, and thankful. Forgive me for slacking off in prayer and being lazy or slow to come to You. God, I recommit my heart, my priorities, and my posture so I can be devoted to prayer. From this day forward, I lay down every excuse at Your feet and I will to devote myself in prayer. In the name of Jesus, I pray. Amen.

My Affirmation

I will be vigilant and pray.

#dwellhere

DAY 9

Today's Scripture

1 PETER 3:12, NIV

For the eyes of the Lord are on the righteous and his ears are attentive to their prayer, but the face of the Lord is against those who do evil.

The Righteous

The most significant element about the sacrificial death of Jesus is that it restored God's direct connection to us. Now, we have the opportunity to have an audience with the Almighty God through prayer. However, there is a condition of righteousness that evokes God's attentiveness. We need God's ears to be attentive to our prayers. Righteous doesn't mean without sin. Righteousness speaks to the purity of heart and rectitude of life, which simply means being right and doing right. We want God's eyes and ears but not His wrath or face. Evil should be far from the believer's heart. In your quest to becoming a dwelling place for God, seek God's eyes and ears through righteous living. Let's not take God's grace nor redemptive plan for granted by living with sin, unrighteousness, hardness of heart, unforgiveness, or anything else that would hinder our prayers from God's ears.

#dwellhere

Pray the Word

Precious God, I thank You for Your Word that encourages, admonishes, and teaches. Father forgive me for every sin of commission or omission that separates me from You. Forgive me for every time You couldn't be attentive to my prayers because of my unrighteousness. God, I pray, that I will keep my heart, my mind, and life in such a righteous way that I will always be seen and heard by You. I submit my life to You, and my will to be righteous, to be good, and do good. God you are merciful and for that I am blessed to be in relationship with You.
In Jesus' name, dwell here. Amen.

My Affirmation

I am righteousness.

#dwellhere

DAY 10

Today's Scripture

PSALM 24:3-4, NIV

Who may ascend the mountain of the Lord? Who may stand in His holy place? The one who has clean hands and a pure heart, who does not trust in an idol or swear by a false god.

A sacred place or thing, sanctity, consecrated, dedicated.

#dwellhere

Entry to the Holy Place

In order for us to be where God is, our heart and our hands must be pure before Him. We can appear clean and pure in front of people because of the world's standards, however, being clean and pure of heart is a whole different truth. God sees, God knows, God doesn't have to discern or try to figure out if you are clean. God knows. We spend a lot of time trying to impress people with clothes, houses, money, titles, and platforms which easily can become idols. None of which is impressive to God who sees you and knows you better than yourself. In order to become and remain a dwelling place for God, it must be with clean hands and a pure heart. As you lift your hands and your heart in worship, they should be free from malice, sin, and unforgiveness. And full of love, righteousness, holiness, and meekness.

What do you need to let go of to enter God's holy place? What do you need to remove from your house, natural or spiritual for God to enter? Today, is a good day to clean your house and enter God's place.

#dwellhere

Pray the Word

God, my desire is to be where You are. My heart yearns to be present in Your midst, but I know I cannot do that any-old-kind-of-way. God, clean my hands and my heart. Wash me that I may be pure. Reveal to me areas that are hidden from man but visible to You so that I may walk blameless before You. When I present my heart and my hands in worship God, they will be clean. I denounce and pull down any idol in my life. Forgive me for placing any thing or any person before You. It's by Your grace alone that I am here, therefore, I will be clean and pure so that I can dwell with You, in Jesus' name. Amen.

My Affirmation

I shall be clean and pure.

#dwellhere

DAY 11

Today's Scripture

JOHN 15:10, NKJV

If you *keep* My commandments, you will abide in My love, just as I have kept My Father's commandments and abide in His love.

To guard from loss or injury by keeping an eye on

#dwellhere

Guard!

Jesus was sent to live on Earth and demonstrated how we are to walk and live our lives in this place. In the words of Christ, He admonishes us to do what He did in obedience to God our Father, as it keeps us in God's love. Jesus identifies the glue that connects us to God, and His love is our obedience. It is through our obedience to God's Word and voice that we remain in His love. If you desire to be the dwelling place of God and be dwellable, then you must be obedient. Your obedience is the key to remaining in God's love. Obedience is for your own good, and for His love. Jesus says, "just as I..." He is not asking us to do anything He has not done. Keep guard, and obey the commands of our Lord and bask in His everlasting love.

We guard the things that we love. We keep the things that we love close to us. When we keep the commandments, we keep His love close and we become dwellable.

#dwellhere

Pray the Word

Gracious God, thank You for the example of Your son Jesus. Thank You for sending Jesus as a Savior, example, and a model for us. Forgive me for every time I've strayed away from Your voice and disobeyed Your Word, whether through commission or omission. God, I want to live in You, and I want You to live in me. I want to remain in Your love. Help me to remove anything in my life that would separate my heart from Your love. Above all, God I'm thankful for You being close, available, and near to me in the name of Jesus I pray, dwell here. Amen.

My Affirmation

I will remain in God's love.

#dwellhere

DAY 12

Today's Scripture

JOHN 14:23, NKJV

Jesus answered and said to him, "If anyone loves Me, he will keep My word; and My Father will love him, and We will come to him and make Our home with him.

keep — To attend to carefully, take care of, to guard, to observe

home — a staying, abiding, dwelling, abode

#dwellhere

The Key to Our Place

Love is equivalent to obedience in God's dwelling place. This seems strange in our human understanding if we are being honest. But when it comes to God the Father and God the Son, there is no sin, only righteousness. Therefore, obeying the teachings of Christ is for our own good and it demonstrates alignment and agreement with the One whom we obey. When we adhere, respect, and do what Christ has taught us to do, God finds a home with us.

According to Jesus, being a dwelling place for God requires us to be a keeper of the Word of God. The entry gate to our dwelling place is the love of God through our obedience or attending carefully to what we are asked to do. Being a dwelling place, we have to be a keeper of God's word and be diligent in doing what Jesus wants us to do in the earth. Therein lies God's access and key to our dwelling place, and a place where God can feel at home.

#dwellhere

Pray the Word

Gracious God, I long to be a dwelling place for You. Thank You, Jesus, for Your life and the sacrifice that ripped the veil and restored our relationship with the Father. I know You love me because You spared me, therefore obedience is the only right way. Forgive me Father for every time I've disobeyed and strayed. Thank You for bringing me into a relationship with You. Thank You for Your love towards me. I shall obey Your word and Your voice, and I will become a dwelling place for You Lord. I will be a place where You can stay and remain because I will do what You have called me to do in the earth. I will be what You called me to be. Dwell here, with me, in Jesus' name. Amen.

My Affirmation

I will obey.

#dwellhere

DAY 13

Today's Scripture

2 TIMOTHY 2:15, NIV

Do your best to present yourself to God as one approved, a worker who does not need to be ashamed and who correctly handles the word of truth.

Acceptable, approved, tried

#dwellhere

Approved Worker

We are all called to be an approved worker. This is the charge for every believer of the Gospel of Christ. The qualifications of an approved worker lie in our personal presentation to God. When you look at the full context of this scripture, it's clear that we are to be fruitful and truthful communicators of God's Word. We should avoid creating arguments and being a part of the problem in this current world. Being a diligent student of God's Word will position us to be presentable to God and an employee of the Kingdom whom God deems acceptable.

However, creating or adding to chaos around you or on social media with your careless or quarrelsome words discredits your voice. Personally, it grieves my heart when I see people misrepresenting God's character or heart. Our eternity will be spent in heaven, but our work is done here in the earth. When you study the scriptures for yourself, you can stand on God's truth in a bowing world gracefully. Let's be approved by God, not humankind. Posture yourself into a dwellable position and be approved by God.

#dwellhere

Pray the Word

Gracious God, I love You and thank You for this life. I thank You for teaching us how to handle the Word of God and YOUR people with care and diligence. Thank You for leaving us with history, instructions, correction, and Your heartbeat through this living Word. God I will study to show myself approved by rightly handling Your Word, and not drawing upon my flesh, nor mishandling Your truth. God, I want to present myself to You, approved, unashamed, and acceptable to You God as Your dwelling place, I will be diligent in being an approved worker in Your Kingdom while here on earth.

My Affirmation

I am approved by God.

#dwellhere

DAY 14

Today's Scripture

HEBREWS 4:12, NIV

For the word of God is alive and active. Sharper than any double-edged sword, it penetrates even to dividing soul and spirit, joints and marrow; it judges the thoughts and attitudes of the heart.

Discerns, tracing out and passing judgment on the thoughts of the mind

#dwellhere

Surgery of the Heart

I don't think we realize how powerful the Word of God is until we read this text. The Word of God is *alive*. Not only is it alive, but it judges thoughts and hearts. How? The Word of God is alive and active. God's Word is not an inanimate object. God breathed on His Word just as He breathed onto Adam. God's Word is sharp and divinely divisive. However, it has been wrongfully used as a weapon in past generations to control and degrade marginalized people. In the wrong hands with improper use, the Bible is dangerous. I know that's a hard concept for some to grasp. It is the WORD that does the judging and discerns the thoughts and attitudes of the heart. If you mishandle the Word of God, you will in fact mishandle the people of God. Anytime you USE the Bible to mistreat people, your motives are exposed.

The spiritual surgery that takes place with the living Word of God is personal. You submit yourselves to surgery and not try to perform it on others. Flesh is not sustainable in God's dwelling place. The dwelling place is a surgical place, make no doubt about that.

Pray the Word

Gracious God, I thank You and praise You for Your word. You did not leave us alone when we were separated from You, but You've given us Your word, and the Holy Spirit. You remind us that You are Your word – alive and active in the lives of Your people. Your word corrects, instructs, and judges. God let me be found righteous in Your eyes and my motives pure. I pray that I will always handle Your Word as truth, with care, and act accordingly. You are the Living Word and Your Word shall live in me.
In Jesus' name, dwell here, Amen.

My Affirmation

God's Word lives in me.

#dwellhere

DAY 15

Today's Scripture

MATTHEW 4:4, NIV

Jesus answered, "It is written: 'Man shall not live on bread alone, but on every word that comes from the mouth of God.'"

Rhema - that which is or has been uttered by the living voice, thing spoken.

#dwellhere

A Dwellable Diet

The Word of God is alive and when God speaks through God's oracles, through song, exhortation, or prophecy it nourishes our soul. In order to become a dwelling place for God our diet must include God's living Word. Earthly bread adds unwanted calories to our bodies, but living bread adds weight to the indwelling Spirit. My mother used to always say to me, whatever you feed, that's what will grow.

Here's the focus, Jesus said, "every" word that comes from God which means we can't pick and choose what we want to eat or obey as it relates to God's word. We cannot choose a convenient diet. In a time where we can get anything we need "on demand" we have to be aware of what we are selecting to receive both naturally and spiritually. Are there sermon topics that you won't listen to because it makes you uncomfortable or challenges your lifestyle, belief system, or theology?

Jesus was free from sin as He ate every Word that came from His Father. As a dwelling place for God you must consume God's Word daily to live and be livable.

#dwellhere

Pray the Word

Gracious God, I thank You and praise You for being my daily bread. Thank You for every word that You have spoken to me. I pray that I will increase my daily bread and my intake of Your word so that I can be strong in You and more obedient to Your voice. With a daily diet of Your Word my spiritual senses will be strong and my joy complete. Give me this day, my daily bread and I shall be more like You. In Jesus' name, dwell here, Amen.

My Affirmation

I will eat God's word daily.

#dwellhere

DAY 16

Today's Scripture

COLOSSIANS 3:5, NIV

Put to death, therefore, whatever belongs to your earthly nature; sexual immorality, impurity, lust, evil desires and greed, which is idolatry.

#dwellhere

Slay

We were created by God and for God, not for this earth to dwell forever. However, it's hard for us as humans in a human world to combat all earthly desires and issues. But if we don't kill or slay our fleshly desires we are living in idolatry which means there is no room for God. Lust – no. Sexual impurity – no. Greed – no. God can't dwell in us alongside any idol we've erected in our lives. We tend to believe idols are gold statues or inanimate objects. An idol is anything that you make bigger than God in your life. This includes everything and anyone we exalt, place higher, or idolize. We must work on killing what cannot live with God if we want to be a dwelling place for God.

When we invite guests to our home, especially on special occasions, we'll clean it up and make certain our homes are inviting and presentable. In the same manner, we have to remove anything from ourselves that would uninvite or disqualify us from God coming into our lives to dwell.

Pray the Word

Gracious God, I come to You as humble as I can. First giving You honor and praise for my earthly life. Remove any desires in me that do not bring You glory. Slay my flesh Lord. Cleanse me, wash me daily, so that I will live lust free, sin free, and impurity free. Remind me daily that I am a citizen of the Kingdom although a resident of this world. Forgive me for all the evilness in my heart and mind and renew me afresh. Thank You for extending Your mercy to me. Thank You, heavenly Father, for another chance today to live for You, in Jesus' name, dwell here. Amen.

My Affirmation

I will slay my flesh.

DAY 17

Today's Scripture

JEREMIAH 15:16, NKJV

Your words were found, and I ate them,
And Your word was to me, the joy
dabar
and rejoicing my heart; For I am called by
Your name, O Lord God of hosts.

summon, invite

#dwellhere

Joy Through it All

On my worst days and best days God's word lifts me and gives me joy. When everything else in your life feels unstable and inconsistent, rest assured the joy of God's word is available to you. Why? Because God calls us to that joyful place. There is not a place that God's joy cannot reach. We are His and we are called by God's name. If that doesn't make you rejoice nothing else will. Allow God to bring you to a place of joy and watch God dwell with you in that place. In my most difficult seasons, when I read scriptures, they elevated my mood and often changed my attitude toward the situation. One scripture, one passage of text made the biggest difference even on my most difficult day. Whether it is grief, distress, hurt, or disappointment ,God's word will find a way to bring you joy.

Pray the Word

Gracious God, thank You for allowing Your word to be a place of joy in my heart. God in my darkest days, help me to find a place of joy. Allow my heart to rejoice with every comforting word. Reveal to me a dabar word that speaks to my very condition. And most of all, You are invited to dwell with me in my joyful place. In Jesus' name, dwell here. Amen.

My Affirmation

I have joy.

#dwellhere

DAY 18

Today's Scripture

I TIMOTHY 4:7-8, NIV

Have nothing to do with godless myths and old wives' tales; rather, train yourself to be godly. For physical training is of some value, but godliness has value for all things, holding promise for both the present life and the life to come.

→ worldly (annotation on "godless myths")
→ exercise vigourosly (annotation on "train yourself")
→ reverence, respect, piety towards God (annotation on "godliness")

#dwellhere

Training For Service

Being godly as imperfect humans does not come easy. Today, we focus on being godly v. godless. As a child of God, how can we be godlier in a world that doesn't honor the things of God? Most well-trained athletes are in good health. Are you a Christian in good health spiritually? It's through vigilant exercise that we train ourselves. Anything we desire to be good at requires discipline, training, and self-sacrifice. Our minds are inundated with godless music, entertainment, and conversations daily. We must train our hearts and our spirits to reject the things that are not from God, and that would cause us to believe myths and false doctrine. Train your ear to hear God's voice. Discipline yourself to discern God's voice and heart in all matters. Read God's word for revelation and encouragement. Just like with bodily exercise, repetition is the key to strength and growth. Creating a space in your life to be intentional with your spiritual growth is so vital as a believer. When we have done this, we become fit for service and of course...dwellable.

#dwellhere

Pray the Word

Gracious God, I thank You for another day to behold Your promises. Thank You for Your word that teaches me how to train my mind to be Godly – to be more like You every day. You are the truth. Your word is true, and I can train with the assurance that it is for my benefit and my good. Forgive me Father for every time that I've listened to tales rather than Your word. Clean me and purify me of all unrighteousness so that
I may be Godly and carry Your glory
with me at all times.

My Affirmation

I am trained for this.

#dwellhere

DAY 19

Today's Scripture

2 TIMOTHY 1:14, NIV

Guard the good deposit that was entrusted to you – guard it with the help of the Holy Spirit who lives in us.

↪ *to dwell in, to inhabit*

Through the idea of isolation, to watch, be on guard - implies to preserve, obey and avoid.

#dwellhere

The Guard

Every God-thing that exists within us needs guarding. The part of Godself that was deposited in you, needs to be kept guarded as the Bible suggests. However, anything of value to God becomes a target for our adversary. Do not think it strange when the enemy tries to come after you when you are truly living for God. His purpose is to steal, kill, and destroy. The beautiful part is that you don't have to do it alone. The Holy Spirit will help you preserve that which has been deposited in you. This is what we need to sustain us and the very thing we need to guard. The Holy Spirit is indeed a keeper and when we are kept by the Holy Spirit, He dwells in us. The old church mothers used to say, "He's a keeper, if you want to be kept." God has placed His gifts, purpose, and Spirit on the inside of us. Guard it because it is all valuable and necessary to His will.

Your destiny and those who are attached to you are counting on you to guard what God has placed in you. You have been called to fulfill purpose. Guard what God has placed in you to fulfill that. Guard your dwelling place.

#dwellhere

Pray the Word

God thank You for being a keeper. Keep me from all transgressions. Keep me from doing evil in Your sight. Keep me from harming myself and others. Let there be a guard on my mouth, on my eyes, and on my Spirit. God I will guard, preserve, and keep that which has been deposited in me. I will guard everything that You have placed in me to do Your will. Forgive me for every area of neglect that I've left unguarded. Thank You for the Holy Spirit that has been sent to keep me, help me, and to guide me. I will partner with Him to guard my dwelling place. In Jesus' name, dwell here. Amen.

My Affirmation

I shall guard!

#dwellhere

DAY 20

Today's Scripture

COLOSSIANS 3:16, NKJV

Let the word of Christ dwell in you richly *→ logos* in all wisdom, teaching and admonishing one another in psalms and hymns and spiritual songs, singing with grace in your hearts to the Lord.

#dwellhere

Melody of My Heart

When the word of God dwells in you, it should burst in you too. The logos, the word of Christ is given to us and it must be stirred and nurtured through song, psalms, and hymns. You are responsible for knowing the word and living it daily. We should be able to encourage others with the word of God and through songs. Several years ago in a season of grief and trauma, my sister-in-law gave me her iPod with a song list. That song list encouraged me because it nurtured my spirit when I couldn't do the nurturing for myself. Even when you use your social media platforms you can share the gospel with those who don't know Christ. You can encourage hurting and broken hearts with songs and videos to uplift their spirits while glorifying God. As a disciple of Christ, you are responsible for how you use your voice and your platforms. Let the word of God lead you and amplify the voice that echoes the heart of Christ.

There is a sound from heaven that is found in the hearts of God's people. Sing your song in your dwelling place for God. Let the melody of your heart enrich everyone around you.

#dwellhere

Pray the Word

Gracious God, I need Your words to dwell in my heart. Allow Your word to be embedded in my heart through song, melody, and inscription. I will be intentional with my voice and my platform to only glorify You. I will always use the message of Christ to teach, admonish, and encourage those around me from the richness of Your word. Let the words of my heart and the meditation of my heart be acceptable and pleasing to You. In Jesus's name. Amen.

My Affirmation

I will admonish!

DAY 21

Today's Scripture

1 CORINTHIANS 3:16, NIV

Don't you know that you yourselves are God's temple and that God's Spirit (dwells) in your midst?

to remain, abide

#dwellhere

Dwellable

Don't you know? I love this rhetorical question. We were created to be a temple for God to live. Can God live in you? God cannot be joined with carnality, perversion, deception, immorality, etc. Yes, we are all born into sin and shaped in iniquity; however, the salvation of our souls and our blood-washed sins gives us an opportunity to be a dwelling place. This is our re-birth right. We owe it to Jesus, the Son, who died for our sins to make ourselves dwellable. Jesus paid the ultimate price so that we can have a relationship with God, the Father. We are no longer separated from God and He desires not just to live with us, but live in us. Can God live in you? Is He welcomed in your home or in your mind and heart? I encourage you to become dwellable.

#dwellhere

Pray the Word

Gracious God, I am grateful for Your presence, Your plan, and Your purpose for my life. I am truly unworthy of Your presence. Forgive me for all my sins of omission and commission. Throw them into the sea of forgetfulness. God, I desire for Your Spirit to dwell in me. Make me dwellable. Remove everything that is not like You, or that does not bring glory to Your name. I yield my heart, my Spirit, and my body to You God, the everlasting Father, the King of Kings and Lord of Lords, in Jesus' name, dwell here. Amen.

My Affirmation

I am dwellable.

#dwellhere

DAY 22

Today's Scripture

DEUTERONOMY 7:6, NIV

For you are a people holy to the LORD your God. The LORD your God has chosen you out of all the peoples on the face of the earth to be His people, His treasured possession.

↳ sacred, saint, set apart

#dwellhere

The Condition

So many people go through life looking for connection with a desire to belong in a group or with a people. We are His people. This scripture is so full of wonderfulness. It's complete with the plan of God for your life. We are "a" people, called to be holy, chosen out of all the people in the world to be God's people. That is a bountiful blessing and comes with great responsibility and a condition. Holiness is necessary for God's claim on our lives. It is the holy people that are God's people. Yes, we are special and His, but we must also be holy. This is what makes us a treasured possession. As God's dwelling place, and God's people, we must be holy, consecrated, and set apart. This is a condition of the dwelling place.

Pray the Word

Gracious God thank You for the call to holiness and for me to be Your treasured people. Forgive me Lord for not living up to Your standard of holiness and righteousness. Forgive me for every time that I lived beneath the privileges of being God's people. God, I desire to live a holy life and be someone that You can claim as Yours. Help me identify and remove anything that would exalt itself above the holiness of God. Establish Yourself in me God so that I will always be found worthy of the calling to holiness and Your name. In Jesus' name, dwell here. Amen.

My Affirmation

I am His people.

#dwellhere

DAY 23

Today's Scripture

1 PETER 1:15-16, NIV

But just as He who called you is holy,
↳ *to call aloud, to invite*
so be holy in all you do; for it is written

"Be holy, because I am holy."

sacred, set apart

#dwellhere

The Difference

Consider for a moment how we define the opposite of holiness. The words carnality, flesh, and ungodly should all come to mind. The word of God asks us to be holy in all that we do. Failing to be holy in all that we do, ultimately causes us to miss the mark, which is the definition of sin. As born-again believers, our goal, our mark, is holiness. We are charged to be holy, to be set apart for His Kingdom service. We are charged to be holy, and different in all of our actions and in what we consume from media. When we become different, it makes all the difference to God. God wants us to be holy and different.

As a dwelling place for God, your heart, your speech, and your actions should be different from people that do not know God nor serve Him. Be holy, or be different, in all that you do. God cannot dwell in an unholy temple. There is no other choice. Holiness is the right choice and it is what we should desire and strive for daily as a dwellable place.

Pray the Word

Gracious God I thank You for Your word. Thank You for calling me out of darkness and into Your marvelous light. The One who is holy has called for me to be holy. God forgive me for missing the mark. Help me to remove things, behaviors, or habits that are not holy. Help me to improve my speech and even my thoughts so that I may be found holy, different, and set apart. God close the gap from where I miss the mark of true holiness. I will not settle for vain words in my prayers to You that are void of true holiness. I will be a holy, dwellable vessel for You. In Jesus' name. Amen.

My Affirmation

I am holy.

#dwellhere

DAY 24

Today's Scripture

PSALM 91:1, NIV — *covering, hiding, secret place*

Whoever dwells in the shelter of the Most High will rest in the shadow of the Almighty.

— *to remain, abide*
— *shade*
— *to lodge, pass the night*

#dwellhere

Covered and Safe

If you have ever got caught walking in a downpour without an umbrella, you first try to find shelter. You find something that can cover and protect you from getting soaked, and as my grandmother would say "catch a cold". It's only when you go through your personal storm that you really discover God as a Shelter. It's usually not until you need rest that you will see the blessedness of God's shelter. Even outside of a storm, we can rest in God's presence where there is safety.

The shadow, or shade, of God's self, affords us safety from dangers seen and unseen. Through times of civil unrest and pandemics we know that we are safe and covered. We can have peace and rest knowing that the place we sleep is safe and there is no better place to be than in that secret place. This is the place where love abounds, grace is present, and mercy is extended. Once found, we yearn to stay there, dwell-there, remain there, and be found there. God is calling you to that place today.

#dwellhere

Pray the Word

Gracious God, thank You for Your word that illuminates the path to that secret place. A place where I can find intimacy and relationship with You. God, I want to find You in that secret place daily and remain in Your shadow and under Your covering. Thank You for revealing Your secret place to me. Forgive me for every missed opportunity and invitation to come dwell with You in that place. Renew my desire to dwell with You and to be found dwellable. In Jesus' name. Amen.

My Affirmation

I am covered and safe.

#dwellhere

DAY 25

Today's Scripture

ROMANS 8:5, NIV

Those who live according to the flesh have their minds set on what the flesh desires; but those who live in accordance with the Spirit have their minds set on what the Spirit desires.

#dwellhere

Spirit Fed, Spirit Fueled

When you wake up do you grab your phone first? Often, we pick up our phone before our Bible. As we go to work, we may tune in to the radio, TV, or scroll social media channels before we've prayed for the day and talk with God. We are all guilty or have been guilty of days, weeks, or years of this. The reality is, it is easy for our flesh to be fed – it's not as easy for our spirit. It actually doesn't take much effort to feed your flesh with so many carnal choices verses holy choices. Media is not evil nor corrupt, it's a voice. If we are listening to voices that feed our flesh rather than God's spirit within us, then we become carnal and weak.

Being intentional about feeding your spirit requires a will, a desire, and a plan. When your spirit is fed and full it nurtures you and takes care of the things you need spiritually and emotionally. Invite the Holy Spirit to rest, rule, and abide in you daily. When you are Spirit-fed, you will be fueled by the Spirit, you will operate in a way that is pleasing to God, available to God, and dwellable by God.

#dwellhere

Pray the Word

Fill my cup Lord, so that I may overflow. God let Your Holy Spirit dwell and reign in me.
I will not be moved in my flesh.
You are my God and I trust You to live and move in me. Forgive me for my unhealthy diet of the world and create in me a clean heart. Renew my mind Lord and remind me always to live in the Spirit and not remain in this unregenerated flesh.
In Jesus' name, dwell here. Amen.

My Affirmation

I will be fueled by the Holy Spirit.

#dwellhere

DAY 26

Today's Scripture

ROMANS 8:16, NIV

The Spirit Himself testifies with our spirit
↳ *joint witness*
that we are God's children.

#dwellhere

Identify

When the enemy wants us to deviate from our destiny, he will attack us in our identity. The enemy wants to keep you from knowing who you are, and whose you are. If you do not know that you are a child of God, you do not know what kind of power you possess. We do not suffer through life alone. We are joint heirs with Jesus. When life hits hard, don't forget to whom you belong. Don't forget you are a child of the living God. As His child, you are provided for, and covered by your Abba, our Father, in heaven. The Holy Spirit joins with God's Spirit on the inside of you to live through you and faith you through all seasons of life. Rest in knowing that you are His beloved and He desires to dwell with you, His children.

#dwellhere

Pray the Word

Gracious God, the words in the English language do not adequately describe Your majesty and goodness. As I humble myself, as I pray and thank You for the Holy Spirit that lives in me. Thank You for revealing to me who I am in You and what I am called to do. Comfort me and guide me through all seasons of my life. Thank You for the word that reminds me of who I am and who lives in me. God thank You for being everything I didn't know I needed when I needed it the most. You are mine and I am Yours. In Jesus' name, dwell here. Amen.

My Affirmation

I am His child.

#dwellhere

DAY 27

Today's Scripture

PSALM 90:1, NIV

Lord, you have been our dwelling place → *habitation, refuge*
throughout (all) generations.

#dwellhere

Generational Dwelling Place

By design, God has been a dwelling place for all generations. God's love, His faithfulness, and His mercy is everlasting, unfailing, and long suffering. God has and will always be a dwelling place for His children. God is consistently there, consistently available and consistently God. We need to be more consistent with our availability and focus on spiritual matters. Our future generations need to know who God is and be able to trust God and be a dwelling place for God. Our ultimate success as parents is producing adult children who have hearts after God's own heart. Our goal is to model righteousness so that their vices are prayer and fasting and living godly lives. This must be the hope for the next generation. They must be a dwelling place for God and know that God is their ultimate dwelling place.

#dwellhere

Pray the Word

Gracious God, I thank You for being a dwelling place for all generations. Your faithfulness extends beyond me and existed before me. My heart's desire is to be a dwelling place for You, and I will pass on that desire to my children, family, and to those who watch my life. Forgive me for taking Your consistency and faithfulness for granted throughout each generation. I pray that my family and I will be just as faithful with each generation. Thank You for the word that reminds us of Your faithfulness to all generations. Thank You for being our God. In Jesus' name. Amen.

My Affirmation

I will create a generational dwelling place.

#dwellhere

DAY 28

Today's Scripture

1 JOHN 2:14, NIV

I write to you, dear children, because you know the Father. I write to you, fathers, because you know Him who is from the beginning. I write to you, young men, because you are strong, and the word of God lives in you, *→ logos* and you have overcome the evil one. *→ to conquer, to carry off the victory, victorious*

#dwellhere

Overcomer

There is nothing like knowing who you are in Christ. When you have a "knowing" that is based on a personal experience it builds your confidence in Christ. To know Christ is gain, or a win, and to know that the word of God lives in you renders you accountable. As children of God, we must but prepared to live out the knowledge of that word daily. Becoming a daily place for God demonstrates that knowledge of God. God's word lives in you and you have overcome the plot and plan of the enemy. I dare you to proclaim that you are an overcomer, victorious in every area of your life. You are strong because you serve a God who has never lost a battle. The word of God lives in you and positions you to be a dwellable place for God.

#dwellhere

Pray the Word

Gracious God, thank You for being the God of my youth and the God of my children's children. Thank You for every experience that has taught me who You are, whether it was in suffering, or the mountain top of victory. Forgive me for every doubt and/or disobedient step in between. You are the God of my dwelling place and I love You, but so grateful that you loved me first. You have equipped me to be an overcomer, and to walk through each season with grace. I am confident only because I know I am Your child. You are my God; my Father and I pray that one day You say, "Well done." In Jesus name, dwell here. Amen.

My Affirmation

I am an overcomer.

#dwellhere

DAY 29

Today's Scripture

ROMANS 12:1-2, NIV

Therefore, I urge you brothers and sisters, in view of God's mercy, to offer your bodies as a living sacrifice, holy and pleasing to God – this is your true and proper worship. Do not conform to the pattern of this world, but be transformed by the renewing of your mind. Then you will be able to test and approve what God's will is – his good, pleasing and perfect will.

#dwellhere

Transformed

It's no surprise that the world is increasingly becoming more wicked and immoral. Presidents, heads of state, and even some churches do not hold the standard for morality and decency. We cannot look to the world to determine who is right. We have to look to God and His Word which admonishes us to be transformed by the renewing of our mind. We were all born in sin and shaped in iniquity. Therefore, we must be transformed. Our minds and our bodies belong to God. Our true worship is to submit our bodies, ourselves, our minds as a living sacrifice, holy and pleasing to God. When this is done, we are able to discern what comes from God and what does not. If you are not fully submitted, if you haven't been transformed, you cannot fully know God nor His will. Be a dwelling place for God, submit yourself and live transformed

Pray the Word

Gracious God, thank You for my breath of life. Thank You for being a gracious and matchless God. I submit to You, myself as a living sacrifice, holy and pleasing in Your sight. I understand that even my worship begins with a self that has been fully submitted. God forgive me for living from a self-absorbed place instead of a self-less place. Forgive me for every day or season that goes by that I did not submit my body as a living sacrifice. God I will live and be transformed by the renewing of my mind in Jesus' name, dwell here. Amen.

My Affirmation

I am transformed.

#dwellhere

DAY 30

Today's Scripture

EPHESIANS 3:17-18, NIV

...so that Christ may dwell in your hearts through faith. And I pray that you, being rooted and established in love, may have power, together with all the Lord's holy people, to grasp how wide and long and high and deep is the love of Christ...

#dwellhere

Rooted in Love

By reading this devotional, you embarked on a journey to be a dwelling place for God. It is through God's word and daily prayer that your heart searches for God. As you continue the search for God, God will keep looking for you to be a dwelling place. He keeps looking and calling for us. His love envelopes us – its deep, its wide, its long and high, and its available to those who have been rooted and established in this love. When we are rooted and established in His love we are covered, secure, and serious about our spiritual growth and becoming that dwelling place. It all comes back to the one key truth, that God so loved the world that He gave His only Begotten to be a ransom for you and me.

#dwellhere

Pray the Word

Gracious God thank You for the love that You have for me that extends beyond my natural and spiritual eyes. Your love covers my faults, heals my wounds, and corrects my vision. The more I dig into You the more rooted and dwellable I will become. I want to be established and firm in Your word and Your truth. Thank You for reminding me today of my position in Your Kingdom, and in Your heart, and in Your love. God get the glory out of my dwellable life, in Jesus' name, dwell here. Amen.

My Affirmation

I am a dwelling place.

#dwellhere

About the Author

Athena C. Shack, MDiv is an entrepreneur and the author of multiple books, the scripture writing/prayer journal series, Write. Listen. Pray.™ and designer of inspirational stationery. She is an ordained minister of the gospel and international speaker with a passion for the brokenhearted who teaches and proclaims God's power of redemption and restoration. As a business owner, she has a mission to deliver books and resources to the marketplace that refreshes the spirit, renews the mind, and restores the spirit. Her debut book, *Grace for the Journey*, also bears the name of her ministry that empowers believers to overcome life's challenges with the Grace of God in route to their destiny. At the end of the day she's a busy mom of an artsy little lady and two charming boys, and wife to her amazing husband. Connect with her on social media, @Write.Listen.Pray.

#dwellhere

Other Books By Author

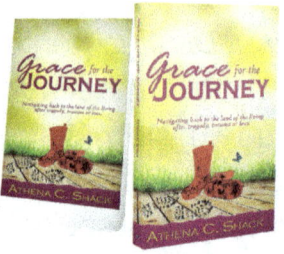

Grace for the Journey: Navigating back to the land of the living after tragedy, trauma, or loss. Published by Watersprings Publishing, sold on Amazon, Barnes & Noble, www.waterspringsmedia.com and everywhere books are sold.

Topical Scripture Writing/Prayer Journals
Write. Listen. Pray.™

Available on www.writelistenpray.com, Amazon, Barnes & Noble, and everywhere books are sold.

#dwellhere

www.ingramcontent.com/pod-product-compliance
Lightning Source LLC
Chambersburg PA
CBHW052115110526
44592CB00013B/1618